# JONAH · RUTH
## A Friend for the Journey

### Carolyn Nystrom

## VICTOR BOOKS

A DIVISION OF SCRIPTURE PRESS PUBLICATIONS INC.
USA   CANADA   ENGLAND

All Scripture quotations are from the *Holy Bible, New International Version®*. Copyright © 1973, 1978, 1984 by International Bible Society. Used by permission of Zondervan Publishing House. All rights reserved.

Poems appearing on pages 18, 25-26, 33, and 39 are reprinted from *You! Jonah!* by Thomas John Carlisle, © 1968 by Wm. B. Eerdmans Publishing Company, used with permission.

Studies on the Book of Ruth incorporate material from *Finding Contentment* by Carolyn Nystrom. Used by permission of InterVarsity Press, P.O. Box 1400, Downers Grove, IL 60515.

Editor: Pamela T. Campbell
Cover Design: Scott Rattray
Cover Photo: Rick Durrance II

Recommended Dewey Decimal Classification: 224.92
Suggested Subject Heading: BIBLE, O.T., JONAH AND RUTH

ISBN: 1-56476-363-3

1  2  3  4  5  6  7  8  9  10  Printing/Year  99  98  97  96  95

# Contents

# Welcome to TruthSeed

I am a planter. Each spring finds me stooped in my garden, loose dirt churned soft by winter storms oozing into my worn sneakers, the smell of compost twitching my nose, warm sun thawing the muscles of my back, and precious seed—radish, carrots, lettuce, peas, beans, corn, beets, watermelon, cantaloupe, squash, cosmos, marigold, zinnia—trickling through my fingers. It's my favorite phase of gardening, one I try to remember as I tug at thick weeds in late June's humidity, swat mosquitoes in sweltering July twilight, and heft baskets of produce into my August-cluttered kitchen. I cut, peel, blanch, can, freeze, and (in recent years) mostly give away—with neighbors and coworkers cashing in on my penchant for planting. It's hard to believe that seeds barely filling a lunch bag spend a few weeks blending God's creative magic of sun, soil, and water into a winter's worth of food for a family. But that's what seed is all about. Abundant life encased in a tiny, hard shell.

No mere book can deliver full-grown, harvested produce—though some come close. Like seeds, books contain a grain of truth encased in the crusty shell of words. But plant that seed in the right season in a mind ready to learn, tug out the weeds of distraction that disrupt study, water it with a sweated-out attempt to put its truths into practice, invite with prayer the sunshine of God's grace, and expect a crop—enough to nurture personal growth, enough to give away.

## What harvest can we expect from TruthSeed?

**We can expect to know Scripture.** Each book in this series invites us to explore either a topic addressed in several biblical passages or to study an entire book of the Bible. These are inductive studies. Each session leads us to explore a single passage on three levels: details of information presented in the text, accurate interpretation of that information, and personal response.

**We can expect to experience God's presence.** Scripture points us to God, its author and its object. It is His letter to us about Himself. As we read, study, and meditate on Scripture we will become more and more aware of God. We will see His love and wrath, His mercy and justice, acted out on the pages of these ancient texts. And we will know more and more about God's personal care for us and His desire for us to respond to Him.

**We can expect to improve our relationships.** Human nature is remarkably resilient; over the millennia we have changed little. Scripture shows us brothers who hate each other enough to kill, and friends who love each other more than their own lives. It shows us the grief of death and the joy of birth. It shows us the celebration of marriage and the pain of marriage ended. It pictures overwhelming generosity and the grudging hunger of greed. It echoes our hopeless moans at life's futility and it shouts our hope for life beyond this life. As Scripture increases our understanding of each other, we can expect to see its fruit wherever we touch other people: at work, in friendships, at churches, in neighborhoods, in casual encounters with waitresses and store clerks, and in the most challenging of all relationships: our families.

**We can expect to better understand ourselves.** Scripture is an intensely personal book. True, we may read it for historical content, or for its quality literature, or for its insightful teachings. But if Scripture is to accomplish its true purpose, we must read its pages, open ourselves, and allow it to read our souls. Scripture will show us our faults: the jealous brother, the greedy servant, the pompous keeper of laws. But as we let Scripture do its work, we will grow more and more according to God's design: the forgiving parent, the faithful leader, the wise friend, the one who models the love of Jesus Christ. And we will find the empty, God-shaped hole inside being filled by Christ Himself. Even people who don't believe much of what the Bible says, who are turned off by sermons and essays, can appreciate the questions here that allow them to examine the biblical text for themselves, explore its potential meanings, and form personal conclusions about response.

TruthSeed is appropriate for small group discussion or for personal use. Its blend of academic, personal, and relational tasks make it ideal for cell groups, workplace study groups, neighborhood groups, school-based groups, Sunday School classes, retreats, and outreach groups. It is also for personal study, meditation, and growth.

## Suggestions for Group Discussion

**1. There's no need to be a Bible expert** to participate in a TruthSeed discussion. You may find experts in your group, but there is plenty of room for non-experts as well. Since the discussion centers around a single passage, you will all participate on a similar level. And God can grow any of us.

**2. Arrive on time** — out of consideration for other group members. Bring your TruthSeed guide and a Bible.

**3. Commit to regular attendance.** Understanding of the Scripture and relationships within the group are cumulative. You and others will benefit most if you can count on each other to be there. If you must be absent, call your host or leader ahead of time.

**4. Discussion is a shared responsibility.** It blends talking and listening in even balance. If you are a born listener, act on your responsibility to share your insights by making the extra effort necessary. If you are a born talker, sharpen your listening skills by keeping track of the flow of conversation. If you discover that you are "on stage" more than the average person present, shorten your comments and use them to draw other people into the conversation.

**5. Treat other group members with respect.** You cannot possibly agree with every comment throughout the course of a discussion study. Disagreement is one way to help each other grow toward the truth. But express your disagreement in kind terms that reflect a genuine respect for the person.

**6. Guard the privacy of people in your group.** Since spiritual growth makes a deep impact on our personal lives, you will likely hear others speak of their private feelings and events. And you may want to speak some of your own private thoughts. Agree together that you will not divulge each other's stories.

**7. Don't gossip.** Many groups pray together for a variety of needy people. It's tempting to get specific about names and weaknesses in a way that invites more speculation than prayer. Don't do it. It's possible to pray for a person with very little inside information. God knows it anyway.

**8. Be willing to discuss the application questions.** Some people are content to keep a group study at a purely academic level, so they read the questions that invite personal response, and pass on with the quick instruction to "think about it." But if Scripture is to be more than a textbook of information, we must allow it to penetrate our lives. Members of a group can nurture each other toward spiritual growth as they discuss together its personal impact.

**9. Take note of the follow-up assignments.** Each TruthSeed study ends with supplementary material that can provide further enrichment. In some cases, this section may prove as valuable as the rest of the study. So take advantage of this added resource.

**10. Consider leading a discussion.** Many groups rotate leadership so that almost everyone takes a turn asking the questions. This job does not require a lot of special skills, but a few pointers won't hurt. If it's your turn to lead, you will find helps for leaders beginning on page 63.

## Suggestions for Personal Study

**1. Settle into your favorite "quiet time" spot.** Bring your Bible, the TruthSeed guide, writing materials, and (if you like) a commentary or Bible dictionary.

**2. Pray.** Ask God to reveal Himself to you as you study. Ask that He assist your understanding, that He bare your inner self to His gaze, and that He use your time to bring healing to your relationships.

**3. Begin by reading the chapter introduction.** Make notes about the first question and allow it to help you approach the topic you are about to study.

**4. Read the assigned biblical text.** If textual accuracy is one of your priorities, use a contemporary translation (not a paraphrase) that reflects recent scholarship. Mark significant words or phrases in your Bible, draw lines between ideas that seem connected, write questions or comments in the margins. Try reading aloud. It's one of the best ways to keep your mind from wandering.

**5. Work through the list of questions.** Jot notes in the space provided. Keep a journal of answers that require more space or more lengthy personal reflection.

**6. Stop for periods of silence and meditation** throughout your quiet time to allow God to work in your inner being.

**7. Continue to pray as you study,** asking God to reveal what He wants you to know of yourself and of Himself. Read aloud sections of the passage as a prayer inserting "I" and "me" where appropriate—or insert the name of someone you care about.

**8. Don't feel that you must do an entire lesson at a single sitting.** Feel free to break at natural division points or whenever you have "had enough" for now. Then come back on a different day, reread the text, review your work thus far, and pick up where you left off.

**9. When you have completed your personal study of the questions, turn to the appropriate leader's notes** in the back of the guide to gain further information you may have missed. If you are the studious type, refer to a commentary or Bible dictionary for more insights. The reading list at the end of the book provides a list of reliable resources.

**10. Put the follow-up activities at the end of each study into practice.** Read, sing, pray, do, meditate, journal, make the phone call, start the project, repair the relationship. When your study time is finished, God's work in your life has just begun. Allow His work to continue throughout the week.

As you use this TruthSeed guide, I pray that seeds of truth from God's Word will grow a rich harvest in your life.

—Carolyn Nystrom, Editor

# Introducing
# Jonah and Ruth

I've always wanted to travel. I've spent most of my life, however, landlocked in the midwest—tightly bound by school, job, and family responsibilities. I'm glad that my work occasions short trips from time to time, and I usually manage to add a day or two of sightseeing to one end or the other. Even when I'm desk-bound, my daydreams take me far away. Leafing through a travel magazine in my dentist's office several years ago led me to plan a fall vacation on the Grand Canyon's north rim. I haven't gotten there yet, but maybe next year. A shell given by a friend sits on my dresser. The tiny inked letters *Aruba* spell another hope, now some ten years old. And how about a winter in Alaska, or a wilderness canoe trip in Wisconsin's north woods? (At least the canoe trip is actually penciled on the calendar.) But I still think longingly of the Canadian Rockies, the Appalachian Trail, and maybe a summer on the New England coast.

Jonah and Ruth were both travelers, though neither enjoyed the luxury of vacation trips. Jonah and Ruth probably lived within 50 miles of each other—but some four centuries apart in time. (Ruth lived first.) Jonah was born among God's people; Ruth was born among their enemies. Jonah traveled alone; Ruth traveled with a companion. Jonah traveled away from God; Ruth traveled toward Him. Both revealed their deepest character during the trip.

Not only do we see human character (sometimes our own) through Jonah and Ruth, we also see the character of God. We see His persistence even with a runaway. We see His compassion for His enemies. We see His patience for a most reluctant student. We see His commitment to a social outcast. We see His kindness to an immigrant. We see His faithfulness to a bitter old woman. God did not abandon either Jonah or Ruth. No matter how much we feel that we choose our own path, we are not really alone. God is our friend for the journey.

# 1
# Wrong Ways and U-Turns

*Jonah 1*

I wonder what inductive Bible study is all about," I grumped as I entered one of our adult Sunday school classes. The bulletin promised twelve weeks on inductive Bible study. I hoped I'd like it. Otherwise, I'd be out the door after a week or two. I'd studied the Bible since I was a child and could find a text to prove most any doctrine I wanted. For me, the Bible was more a weapon than a guide.

I got hooked. In order to demonstrate the various inductive techniques of study, our leader selected the Book of Jonah. Soon I was analyzing—word by word, phrase by phrase—this tiny narrative jewel of the Old Testament. Through that class, I entered an ancient world and got to know a remarkably reluctant prophet named Jonah—and I got to know myself. If I'd been there, I might have worn his name.

The year is 763 B.C., give or take twenty years, and the people of Israel are nervous. The reigning world power, Assyria, is a sprawling empire encompassing today's hot spot of Iraq with tentacles of power reaching northeast to Turkey, south through Saudi Arabia, and southeast to Egypt. Assyrian influence surrounds tiny Israel who is already alienated by civil war from Judah, her sister nation to the south. The people of Israel suffer from aching poverty, internal factions, and war-bought death.

But recent years have brought a breath of relief. Israeli King Jeroboam II is a political success—though a spiritual disaster. He shows every sign of staying in power long enough to bring political and economic stability. The future looks better too. Jonah, a prophet from Gath Helpher, has decreed that God will expand the borders of their little nation—even reach into Assyrian territory near the city of Damascus. And national expansion is beginning to happen.

Best of all, Assyria seems in decline. Her provincial leaders get more attention (and power) than King Ashur-dan III. And King Jeroboam's armies keep nibbling at Assyrian borders.

Six hundred miles to the northeast lies the Assyrian capital city, Nineveh. "Greater Nineveh," extends some 60 miles throughout the region of the Tigris River, but Nineveh itself has shrunk to a mere mile across—populated by some 18,000 people. If this decline continues, perhaps the people of Israel can put more lamb meat in the stew pot and once again sleep without a spear at the bedside.

No one pays much attention to minor military rumblings from a high-culture city 300 miles down river from Nineveh: Babylon. And prophet Jonah, happily cloaked in a welcomed message from God about expanded borders, isn't eager for any other kind of assignment.

1. As you think back over your life thus far, what was your most contented period? What contributed to that era of contentment?

2. What, if any, was the closing point to that era of contentment?

**Read aloud Jonah 1:1-2**
3. Put yourself in Jonah's place. In view of the information in the

introduction to this study, how might you have reacted to Jonah's new assignment? Why?

*Read aloud Jonah 1:3-9*
4. If you were following this story with a video camera, what images and sounds would you want to capture?

5. People view God in a variety of ways. What different views of God do you see in this story? (Consider: the captain, the sailors, the writer of the story, Jonah.)

6. What conflicts do you see between Jonah's stated beliefs about God and his actions?

7. What conflicts have you seen between your own beliefs and actions?

*Read aloud Jonah 1:9-17*
8. What word pictures throughout this chapter help express the violence of this Mediterranean storm?

9. If you had been one of the sailors, how would you have reacted to Jonah's request that you throw him into the sea? Why?

10. What examples of sel*fish*ness and self*less*ness do you see in these events?

11. Once the Phoenician sailors were safely back on shore, what do you think they told their families about Jonah and his God?

12. Three days and three nights inside a fish has long been a subject of controversy and of jokes. How does verse 17 seem to fit with what the Jonah story has said thus far about God?

13. Few of us have experienced a submarine voyage inside a fish, but God *does* use more subtle ways to get our attention. What is one of your own "fish stories"—a time when you were headed the "wrong way" and God used some surprising method to turn you around?

14. What have you learned about yourself and about God from the wrong turns that you have taken?

# Continuing with Worship

## God Moves in a Mysterious Way

1. God moves in a mys - te - rious way His won - ders to_____ per - form; He plants his foot - steps in the sea, and rides up - on the storm.
2. Deep in un - fath - om - a - ble mines Of nev - er - fail - ling skill He treas - ures up his bright de - signs, And works his sov - ereign will.
3. Ye fear - ful saints, fresh cour - age take; The clouds ye so_____ much dread Are big with mer - cy, and shall break In bless - ings on your head.
4. Judge not the Lord by fee - ble sense, But trust him for_____ his grace; Be - hind a frown - ing prov - i - dence He hides a smil - ing face.
5. His pur - pos - es will rip - en fast, Un - fold - ing ev - 'ry hour; The bud may have a bit - ter taste, But sweet will be the flow'r.
6. Blind un - be - lief is sure to err, And scan his work_____ in vain; God is his own in - ter - pre - ter, And he will make it plain. A - MEN.

William Cowper, 1774

HERMON C. M.
Lowell Mason, 1832

## Continuing with Prayer

✦ When Jonah was far from land and about to drown in the sea, he described himself by saying, "I am a Hebrew and I worship the LORD, the God of Heaven, who made the sea and the land." Use Jonah's pattern of a faith statement to form your own personal prayer. Begin, "I am ＿＿＿＿＿＿ *(your name)*, and I worship the Lord who. . . ."

✦ We, like Jonah, sometimes go the wrong way. Admit to God some of your own wrong turns. Thank Him for ways that He has steered you back to the right direction.

✦ Talk to God about your current plans and goals. If you are able to do so honestly, ask God to use your energies for His own purposes—even if it means taking you in some new direction.

### Coming and Going

*The word came*
*and he went*
*in the other*
*direction.*

*God said: Cry*
*tears of compassion*
*tears of repentance;*
*cry against*
*the reek*
*of unrighteousness;*
*cry for*
*the right turn*
*the contrite spirit.*
*And Jonah rose*
*and fled*
*in tearless*
*silence.*

Reprinted from *You! Jonah!* by Thomas John Carlisle, © 1968 by Wm. B. Eerdmans Publishing Company, used with permission.

# 2

# Journey to the Bottom

*Jonah 2*

Last winter, my prayers felt as exciting as dry toast. Small wonder. My usual prayer time was from behind the steering wheel of my Honda wagon as I navigated rush hour traffic down Illinois' Route 64. I chose that time because my schedule hovered around me, as noisy and crowded as the traffic to my right and left. Between work, family, and church responsibilities, my car housed the only privacy I had left. During that period, I discovered that commuting wasn't a bad time to pray. My conversations with God from my car seat were as valid as those from any chapel. But it was a bad *only* time to pray.

So I scheduled myself for a retreat. One of the pieces of literature crossing my desk announced a five-day summer conference high in the Colorado mountains. I wasn't sure whether I'd encounter hours and hours of lecture, or whether I'd get locked into intense time-consuming relationships, or whether the time would be so unstructured that I'd lack needed guidance. But with a swallow of faith and a trusting look at the name of the conference leader—Richard Foster—I signed up.

I needn't have worried. The conference was all that I had hoped for and more. I suspect I will be drawing on all that I learned and experienced there for years to come. But in my memory, one small aspect still stands high: the matter of scheduling. If *I* were planning a conference, I'd put my strongest speaker at the most opportune time—a time when everyone was fully awake, but not yet tired, a time when casual attenders had not yet taken off for some tourist attraction. I'd probably pick 10:00 A.M. Yet, at 10:00 A.M. each day of that conference, all activity stopped for one hour. All talking ceased. The speakers returned to their rooms or to the hiking trails. We all picked up Bibles, backpacks, and water bottles — and headed outdoors to hear the real speaker: God.

Likewise, if *I* were planning a conference, I'd place my most important activity on a key day — not the first day when everyone is still getting oriented, not the last day when people are packing their bags and confirming airline reservations, but probably the next to last day when interest, knowledge, and energy is at its peak. Yet on that day (Thursday), all scheduled activity ceased. We had no speakers, no small group meetings, no worship services, no group meals until evening. By mutual agreement, when we passed each other in the hallways or on the trails, we nodded, smiled, and moved on. It was a day of silence: a day to think, pray, read Scripture, listen to God, even to sleep. (Most of us found time for a nap.)

I gained much from the Renovaré conference. I suppose I will be processing its information and my experiences there for a long time. But the impact of scheduling uninterrupted time for communication with God has changed my prayer patterns. Sure I still pray in my car. But I also plan small, regular blocks of time for solitude. These times clear away the clutter of my life and turn my focus toward God. The prophet Jonah had a startling opportunity for his own time of solitude with God.

1. Suppose you had several days free to think and pray. How would you likely use the time?



   What are some issues that you would want to explore with God?

*Read aloud Jonah 1:17–2:10*

2. Verse 1 begins, "From inside the fish Jonah prayed to the LORD his God." What different phrases does Jonah use to describe his experience in the sea?

3. In view of his condition at this point, what all do you think ran through Jonah's mind as he encountered the fish?

4. In verse 8, Jonah speaks of idols. In view of Jonah's actions up to this point, what changes in himself do you think this statement reflects?

   What does verse 8 suggest about the people of Nineveh?

5. An idol can be anything that we put ahead of God. What idols tempt you to distance yourself from God?

6. Notice each time Jonah speaks of God in his prayer. How does each of these statements help clarify God's character?

7. In chapter 1, the ship captain told Jonah to pray to his God so that the sailors might be saved from the storm. But the text gives no record that Jonah prayed at that point. Finally from the belly of the fish, Jonah was ready to pray. When has one of your own experiences at "the bottom" brought about honest communication with God?

What did you learn about yourself and about God at that time?

8. Look more carefully at Jonah 2:9. What changes do you see in Jonah because of his three days alone with God?

9. In view of the rest of Jonah's prayer, what all do you think he meant by the words, "Salvation belongs to the Lord"?

10. How would you explain the same statement to a friend who wanted to know what you mean by the words *salvation* and *Lord*?

11. Jonah 1:17 says, "But the Lord provided a great fish. . . ." Keeping in mind all of chapter 2, what do you think was the purpose of the fish?

12. Jonah said in verse 9, "What I have vowed, I will make good." In a time of silence, take stock of your own commitment to God. Ask yourself some of the following questions:

   ✦ Am I sure that I am part of God's family? If not, what is one step I can take in that direction?

◆ What is good about the current quality and quantity of my praying? How might I improve it?

◆ Is my commitment to my church one that allows me to learn, worship, serve, and be served? How can I express my satisfaction with my church or improve my relationship with it?

◆ What steps am I taking to "hear God" through Scripture? If this is inadequate, what changes am I willing to make?

◆ How willing am I to obey God? What is one large or small "mission" from God that I have refused to obey, or obeyed with reluctance?

Make notes below about one area that you would like to emphasize in the near future.

## Continuing with Worship

### Come, All Christians, Be Committed

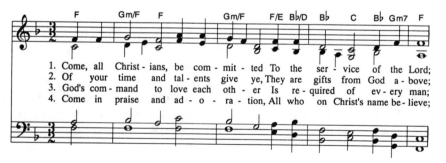

1. Come, all Christ - ians, be com - mit - ted To the ser - vice of the Lord;
2. Of your time and tal - ents give ye, They are gifts from God a - bove;
3. God's com - mand to love each oth - er Is re - quired of ev - ery man;
4. Come in praise and ad - o - ra - tion, All who on Christ's name be - lieve;

Make your lives for Him more fit - ted, Tune your hearts with one ac - cord.
To be used by Christ-ians free - ly To pro - claim His won - drous love.
Show - ing mer - cy to a bro - ther Mir - rors His re - demp - tive plan.
Wor - ship Him with con - se - cra - tion, Grace and love will you re - ceive.

Come in - to His courts with glad-ness, Each His sa - cred vows re - new,
Come a - gain to serve the Sav - ior, Tithes and of-f'rings with you bring.
In com - pas - sion He has giv - en Of His love that is di - vine;
For His grace give Him the glo - ry, For the Spir - it and the Word,

Turn a - way from sin and sad - ness, Be trans - formed with life a - new.
In your work, with Him find fa - vor, And with joy His prais - es sing.
On the cross sins were for - giv - en; Joy and peace are ful - ly thine.
And re - peat the gos - pel sto - ry 'Til all men His name have heard.

Eva B. Lloyd

BEACH SPRING
"The Sacred Harp"
Harmonized by James H. Wood

Fred Bock. *Hymns for the Family of God* (Nashville: Paragon Associates, Inc.) 1976. Page 507. Used by permission.

## Continuing with Prayer

✦ When Jonah tried to run from God, God pursued him — even into the Mediterranean. Thank God for His times of faithfulness to you, particularly for His persistence during those times when you tried to distance yourself from Him.

✦ Confess to God any continued reluctance to fully obey Him.

✦ In view of your self-examination in question 12, are there promises that you want to make to God? If so, make these commitments now in prayer.

✦ Most of Jonah's prayer is a statement of who God is. Praise God in prayer for qualities that you most appreciate.

### Inside the Sea Monster

*I was as low as I could get
when I remembered
God.*

*Odd
that my distress
impressed me with His apparent absence*

*when His promised daily presence
hadn't meant a blessed
thing.*

*Finding
myself in that hole
with my soul fainting, and rolling*

*with the swell of my swollen ego*
*was enough to kill me*
*good.*

*Instead*
*I saw stars in the dark*
*and started home on a welcome waterspout.*

Reprinted from *You! Jonah!* by Thomas John Carlisle, © 1968 by Wm. B. Eerdmans Publishing Company, used with permission.

# 3
# Second Chances

*Jonah 3*

In his classic story, *A Christmas Carol,* Charles Dickens wrote of Ebenezer Scrooge, a selfish, angry owner of a "counting house." Scrooge tortures his long-suffering employee, Bob Cratchit, with low pay, long hours, cold temperatures, and a single, grudged holiday a year. On his current path, Scrooge has doomed himself to a friendless life and a lonely grave. And he will destroy hapless people in his path including Bob Cratchit's child-saint son, Tiny Tim.

But Scrooge gets a second chance — not that he needs one by his own calculations. The ghosts of Christmas past, present, and future reveal to Scrooge (and Dickens' readers) the reasons for Scrooge's anger — hidden in his childhood. The ghosts also show the results of Scrooge's enforced servitude in Bob Cratchit's home. And they point the trembling Scrooge to his final end — and the end of Tiny Tim.

"Are these the shadows of things that *will* be, or are they shadows of things that *may* be, only?" Scrooge pleads, ready to make amends if any hope remains for a changed future. The final ghost makes no such promise. He simply retreats into the shadows leaving Scrooge gasping himself awake as he clutches his bedpost. But the ghosts have done their work in a single night. Scrooge welcomes Christmas morning full of new perspective and new resolve. It's an exuberant story retold each Christmas in television cartoons, in literature classes, and in storybooks illumined by firelight. Everyone loves a second chance, and Scrooge made the best of it.

God has blessed our lives full with second chances. We receive second chances in marriage, in parenting, in school, in finances, in faith, even in driving. One of my own second chances came after two successive miscarriages. I was weak, tired, sad, and angry at God. For the past decade I had filled my schedule full with teaching second graders, giving birth to and caring for our two young daughters, and various responsibilities common to all homemakers. I left little time to nurture my faith. At one point I would have said "Bah! Humbug!" to all things more overtly Christian than church attendance.

My second chance at growing faith came in the form of a spry, graying lady named Lenore. During my weeks of bedrest, while trying to save a doomed pregnancy, Lenore brought me light lunches and thought-provoking Christian books. When the pregnancy ended, she invited me to a prayer group of Bible study leaders. Even though I felt more like staying home and crying all day, she kept inviting me over and over until I found it less depressing to say *yes* than to think up one more excuse for *no*. That group introduced me to fun-loving, intelligent women who were serious enough about their faith to talk about it and as natural about prayer as about laughter. I grew, and so did my faith.

Months later, God also gave me a second chance at becoming a parent again. We took in foster children by the bushel, eventually adopting two boys who were unable to return home.

1. Describe a time when you were given a second chance. What did you do with it?

### *Read aloud Jonah 3:1-10*
2. Focus on Jonah 3:1-2. In what ways are these words similar to the opening words of the book? Why?

3. What signs of repentance do you see in this chapter? (Find all that you can.)

4. Notice Jonah's actions in Jonah 3:3-4. What changes had to take place in Jonah in order to for him to act in these ways?

5. Even though the text does not explain Jonah's motives, verse 3 begins, "Jonah obeyed the word of the LORD. . ." When are you likely to obey God because of obligation rather than genuine desire to do what He requires?

   What is good and what is not so good about this kind of obedience?

6. Study the actions of the Ninevites in verses 5-9. What effects did Jonah and his message have on the people of that city?

7. In view of Jonah's message and Nineveh's response, why did the people of Nineveh need to repent? (See also Jonah 1:2.)

8. What did the people of Nineveh have to believe about Jonah and about God in order to do all that is described here?

9. In what appropriate ways do people today show repentance?

10. Why should we repent of anything? (When we repent, what are we saying about ourselves? About God?)

11. Look again at the king's decree in verse 9. How did his understanding of God contribute to caution but also to hope?

12. Verse 9 presents two opposing aspects of God's character. How do you acknowledge both of these opposite qualities of God in your own thinking? In your behavior?

13. The closing verse of this chapter ends with God's compassion. He not only gave Jonah a second chance, He extended that same opportunity to the people of Nineveh. Did God change His mind? Explain.

**14.** What circumstances in your life make you thankful for God's compassion?

**15.** People who belong to God become more and more like Him. What are one or two situations, now part of your life, where you can show a God-like compassion? How?

## Continuing with Worship

### Humble Thyself in the Sight of the Lord

Bob Hudson

Bob Hudson

## Continuing with Prayer

✦ Thank God for ways that you have seen His compassion.

✦ Mention to Him some of the second chances that He has given to you and thank Him for those opportunities.

✦ Sometimes repentance is the avenue to God's second chance — as it was with Jonah and with the people of Nineveh. Take time now to silently repent to God for any wrong that you know separates you from Him.

✦ In your prayer, speak the names of one or two people who need your compassion. Ask God to show you ways to better express His kind of mercy.

### Limitation

*God changed His mind*
*because they had changed*
*their hearts.*
*He repented*
*because they repented.*
*That is the way*
*we word it*
*sometimes.*
*But always*
*He is limited*
*only by*
*His limitless love.*

Reprinted from *You! Jonah!* by Thomas John Carlisle, © 1968 by Wm. B. Eerdmans Publishing Company, used with permission.

# 4
# The Uncontrollably Compassionate God

*Jonah 4*

There's a guy in prison who's written a book I'd like you to look at," said Doug Coe to a new acquaintance at an early morning prayer meeting.

Publisher Len LeSourd, trying to get a new book company off the ground, was skeptical. The last thing his fledgling book company needed was a book by some jailhouse convert trying to get a reduced prison term by claiming that he'd gotten religion. And this particular prisoner had a long and nasty reputation.

Reluctantly, LeSourd agreed to a meeting. He sat down with the prisoner; a guard waited outside the door. A halting conversation began. The manuscript proposal had already been rejected many times — one more red flag in the long line of objections. Abruptly the prisoner stopped the conversation: "We have to pray about this," he said.

"You can tell something about a person by the way he prays," LeSourd said later, "and this guy was real." By the time the meeting was over, LeSourd was willing to risk the reputation of his new company on an unpublished prisoner. Other publishers were convinced LeSourd had made a mistake — and that they had avoided one.

"All through the time we were working on this book we had nothing but bad vibes from all kinds of people who'd heard we were doing the book," says LeSourd. Even *he* worried about the welfare of his company as he prepared for critics to pounce on the new text.

But skeptical Christians were in for a surprise. *Born Again* became a bestseller, and more than two decades later, Charles Colson remains an articulate spokesman for the Christian faith.

By some perverse logic, we Christians can sing with tears in our eyes:

> *Amazing grace! how sweet the sound—*
> *That saved a wretch like me!*
> *I once was lost but now am found,*
> *Was blind but now I see.*

Yet when we come across a real *wretch,* not a wretch "like me," but a wretch who actually went to jail, we get tempted to put limits on God's amazing grace. *God's compassion is for nice people,* we think. How could God save a wretch like Charles Colson? Or the people of Nineveh?

1. When have you appreciated someone accepting you?

**Read aloud Jonah 3:10–4:11**

2. If you had not read this story before, what would surprise you about the events in this chapter?

3. Why, according to Jonah, did he run away to Tarshish? (Do you believe him?)

4. Study Jonah's description of God in the second half of verse 2. Why do you appreciate these qualities of God?

5. What do you know about yourself that causes you to appreciate God's compassion?

6. Why do you think that Jonah stayed around Nineveh after he had finished preaching?

7. If Jonah's prayers could have controlled God, what do you think he would have prayed at this point? With what results?

8. Jonah referred several times in this book to his death. (See Jonah 1:12; 2:2, 6; 4:3, 9.) What do these references imply about the way Jonah felt about his life—and his death?

9. Not everyone experiences the kind of death wish that Jonah expressed, but most people experience disappointments that cause them (at least temporarily) to find little joy in life. What are some of the healthy ways that you have coped with life-numbing disappointments?

10. How has God taken care of you during those disappointing times?

11. Twice God asked Jonah, "Do you have any right to be angry?" How would you answer that question for Jonah?

12. Why do you think God provided Jonah with a vine, a worm, and the wind?

13. What could Jonah have learned about himself, about God, and about Nineveh from this final conversation with God?

14. It has been said, "Jonah is Everyman." What do you see of yourself in Jonah? How can you benefit from Jonah's story?

15. The Book of Jonah does not end with Jonah; it ends with God. What characteristics of God do you find revealed in this book? (Draw from the entire book.)

## Continuing with Worship

### Be Still and Know

Verses 1 and 2, ANONYMOUS
Verses 3 and 4, TOM FETTKE

ANONYMOUS
*Arranged by Lee Herrington and Tom Fettke*

## Continuing with Prayer

✦ Take a few moments to be silent. Use this time to acknowledge God's presence. Bring to mind all of those qualities that you know to be true of His character.

✦ Even though Jonah was angry at God, he acknowledged correctly who God is. Pray sentence prayers of praise that name the qualities of God. For example, "I praise You, God, because You are . . ."

✦ We cannot choose where God will exercise His compassion. That is up to Him alone. Thank God for those times that you have seen His mercy and compassion at work.

✦ Bring before God the names of those people whom you hope will receive His mercy and compassion. You can begin, "God, be merciful to . . ."

✦ Survey ways that Jonah's story has touched your own life. Talk to God about these.

### Reprimand to a Naive Deity

*I will not advertise*
*this crazy scheme*
*of Yours.*

*God, what a farce*
*that men should sin and find*
*escape.*

*I mean, of course,*
*not me*
*but all our mutual*

*antagonists.*
*Dear God, kind God, don't listen*
*to their prayers.*

Reprinted from *You! Jonah!* by Thomas John Carlisle, © 1968 by Wm. B. Eerdmans Publishing Company, used with permission.

# 5

# Loving and Letting Go

I have a son-in-law. But my daughter, his wife, is dead. It is small wonder that I feel kinship with Naomi in the Book of Ruth.

Like Ruth, our son-in-law has treated our family with the greatest consideration since Sheri's death two years into their marriage. But I remember with a pang the first time he introduced me by name, without the added title "my mother-in-law." Yet how can a young single man have a mother-in-law? And why should every casual introduction include the tragic story that explains that occurrence? (I have since learned that "family friend" is an alright title for such occasions.)

Like Naomi, I too grieve for lost grandmotherhood. Our daughter was pregnant with our first grandchild when a car/truck crash killed her — and the child. The picture of a sandy-haired baby with *his* intelligence, and *her* musical talent, wrapped in *my* hand-stitched quilt, rocked to sleep in *our* three-generations-old rocking chair, died that same morning. I am bereft of both daughter and progeny.

But like Ruth and Naomi, our family has discovered, in this tree stump of an in-law relationship, a large measure of love. It is not a love of marriage vows. Those no longer apply. It is not a love of family name. That, too, is different. It is not a love rooted in history. Our history together began in adulthood. It is a love of choice. Will our choice to love carry us through a future marriage or future children? It is too soon to say. But the Book of Ruth gives me hope.

1. Name one in-law related to your family. What do you especially appreciate about that person?

***Read aloud Ruth 1***

2. If you were to paint a portrait of Naomi at this point in her life, what would you try to capture? How?

3. What disasters led Naomi to speak the words of verse 20?

4. How did time and geography contribute to the family's hardships?

5. What events in your own life could have led you to think words similar to what Naomi said at the end of this chapter?

6. Focus on verses 8-9. Why might these words have been difficult for Naomi to say? Why was it important for her to say them?

7. In what ways did Naomi express love for her daughters-in-law?

8. What forms of letting go have you had to accomplish in your own family or friendships?

9. What are some ways that family members or friends can let go, but still express love?

10. What cost was Ruth willing to pay for her love of Naomi?

11. Do you fault Orpah for her decision? Explain.

12. Study more carefully verses 19-22. What all do these verses reveal about Naomi's homecoming?

13. What was Naomi's understanding at this point of God's work in her life?

14. Suppose that you did not know the rest of Naomi's story, but you know your own experience with God. How would you answer her complaint of verses 20-21?

# Continuing with Worship

## I Want Jesus to Walk with Me

1. I want Je - sus to walk with me;
2. In my tri - als, Lord, walk with me;
3. When I'm in trou - ble, Lord, walk with me;

I want Je - sus to walk with me;
in my tri - als, Lord, walk with me
when I'm in trou - ble, Lord, walk with me;

all a - long my pil - grim jour - ney,
when my heart is al - most break - ing,
when my head is bowed in sor - row,

Lord, I want Je - sus to walk with me.
Lord, I want Je - sus to walk with me.
Lord, I want Je - sus to walk with me.

Spiritual

WALK WITH ME Irreg.
Spiritual
Arr. by John F. Wilson, 1964; alt. 1990

## Continuing with Prayer

✦ Naomi and Ruth lived in an era of incredible violence. Talk to God about the violence in your own era. Ask His healing and protection for the people involved.

✦ Bring to mind particular situations of turmoil that touch your own life. Ask God to make you an instrument of peace in those situations.

✦ Name each member of your family. For each one, consider in prayer whether you ought to love more, let go more — or both. Ask God's help.

✦ Naomi experienced such severe trauma that it tainted her view of God. Bring to God the disasters of your own life. Ask that in spite of these occurrences He will allow you to see an accurate picture of Himself. If it is appropriate, ask God to heal your faith and enable you to fully trust His love for you.

### Fellow Pilgrim

*Naomi, my sister, my friend,*
*Trudging hollow-eyed*
*The arid waste of grief*
*And barren dreams*
*With Mara-bittered faith.*
*Who's God? Where's God? Is God . . .*
*Walk with us, Jesus.*

— CN

# 6
# Quiet Commitment

*Ruth 2*

The Book of Ruth, with its gentle account of love and fidelity, is set in one of the most violent eras of Hebrew history. The book opens with the words, "In the days when the judges ruled. . . ." So the quiet story of Naomi, Ruth, and Boaz is set in the same era when Ehud faked a message from God for Eglon, King of Moab, then drove a foot and a half sword through the king's belly (Judges 3). A short time later, Jael invited Canaanite King Sisera into her tent, lulled him to sleep, then drove a tent stake through his head (Judges 4). As for the treatment of women, Judges 19 records one of the most gruesome stories in all of Scripture, set (by the way) in Naomi's home town of Bethlehem. The Book of Judges ends with this terse statement of lawlessness: "In those days Israel had no king; everyone did as he saw fit" (Judges 21:25).

Yet, the quiet people of this story did obey certain laws — customs that may seem strange in today's culture, but customs that in those days protected the rights of vulnerable people — especially women who might otherwise receive the violent fate of the pitiable mistress in Judges 19. For poor people like Ruth who arrived in the middle of the harvest season, too late to put in crops even if she owned land, there was the ancient custom of gleaning. The gleaning laws set down by Moses gave landowners some measure of responsibility for the poor who lived and traveled among them. Not that many could have been expected to observe such a financially imprudent custom in an age of lawlessness.

Then there was the strange law of levirate with its "kinsman-re-deemer"—also stemming from the era of Moses. We feel appalled today by the idea that some ancient law would assign a new marriage partner to a widow. But in an era when life itself depended on land ownership and a younger generation to care for the older ones, widowhood was an assignment to poverty, social isolation, lack of legal protection, possible prostitution, and an early death. Under those conditions, an assigned husband was not a bad deal—at least for the woman. For the man, however, it might add to his already heavy legal and financial responsibilities. No wonder he was called a redeemer! And no wonder that Scripture records more men trying to escape this custom, than agreeing to it.

In an era when law was whatever you could get away with, we find a gentle refreshment in the people of Ruth's story. They valued the ancient customs, they cared for the people, and they worshiped God.

1. What are some customs in your own culture, church, or family that you appreciate?

*Read aloud Ruth 2*

2. What all can you know about Boaz from this chapter?

3. What hints do you see that Ruth could be in danger?

4. Naomi described Boaz, in verse 20, as a "kinsman-redeemer." Read Leviticus 25:25-28 and Deuteronomy 25:5-6. In view of these ancient laws from Moses, why did the identity of Boaz bring hope to Naomi?

5. What do you see in this chapter that further reveals the kind of person Ruth is?

6. When Ruth gathered food in someone else's field, she was following the custom of gleaning. Read how that custom began in Deuteronomy 24:19-22. What value can you see to this law?

7. Mentally survey what you know so far about each of the three main people in the Book of Ruth. What is one character quality evidenced by these people that you would like to further develop in yourself?

8. Look closely at the words of Boaz in verse 12. What does this reveal about his understanding of God's nature?

9. Boaz spoke of taking refuge under God's wings. When have you felt protected and loved by God?

10. Notice Naomi's words about God in verse 20. How has her view of God expanded from what she said to her neighbors when she first returned to Bethlehem? (See also Ruth 1:20-21.)

11. When and how have you seen God's kindness during a period of adversity?


12. The people of Ruth's story lived in one of the most violent eras of Hebrew history. What have you seen here that could help you live in a wholesome way in your own society?

# Continuing with Worship

## In My Life Lord, Be Glorified

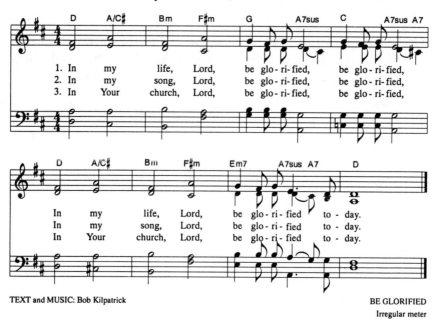

TEXT and MUSIC: Bob Kilpatrick

BE GLORIFIED
Irregular meter

For additional verses, change the word *life* to *work, words, home, school,* etc.

## Continuing with Prayer

✦ Spend a few moments of quiet. Invite God to enter the normal turmoil of your life and soften it with His peace.

✦ Boaz said that Ruth had taken refuge under the wings of God. Allow yourself to sense God's sheltering wings over you. Talk to Him about what that means to you. Thank God for the ways you have experienced His sheltering care.

✦ Mention to God specific areas of unrest in your life (home, church, work, or other). Ask Him to show you ways that you can glorify Him there.

✦ Bring to mind one place in the world that is experiencing violence. Pray for the leaders in that place. Pray for the people there who are trying to live out their faith in spite of their violent surroundings.

### God's Wings

*Does God have wings like an eagle*
*To soar and cut the wind,*
*Or like a butterfly*
*Dusted with rainbow light,*
*Or like a soggy, squatting hen*
*Hunkered to utilitarian shelter?*

*Yes, for me.*

—CN

# 7
# Counting Kindness

*Ruth 3*

I t was a lovely day in early June. Flowering trees laced the warm air with petals caught on a breeze. Violets nestled in newly greened grass. It was the second of the month — the fourteenth monthly anniversary of their first date. (They'd celebrated every one.) He packed drinks, ice, and sandwiches in his styrofoam cooler. She brought a salad. He brought fancy glasses. She brought tableware and napkins. An old blanket from the car would serve as a picnic table.

They found a private nook sheltered by shrubs and munched their picnic lunch. Their hands met from time to time with gentle touch. The breeze tossed playfully through her long blonde hair, her full brown eyes danced with affection.

He took her hand and asked, "What are you going to do with the next sixty years of your life?"

She looked down, confused. Thoughts of school, career, travel, children maybe someday. "I don't know exactly."

"Will you marry me?"

"Yes."

He filled their glasses with ice and sparkling grape. A low-flying helicopter passed overhead, so they toasted the helicopter. They toasted the trees. They toasted their future. Finally, he could wait no longer. "Hey, look in your glass!"

She looked and screeched in laughter. In the bottom of her glass lay a diamond ring. She picked out the ice cube and flung it into the bushes to better reach the ring.

This time her soon-to-be husband was yelling—and diving for the bushes. The ring was not *under* the ice cube, but *in* it.

He retrieved the ice cube. She tried to break or melt the cube to get at its treasure. By now he was yelling, "Careful!" (As if anything could break a diamond.)

In moments the engagement was official and sealed with a kiss. They were off to tell friends and family. It was an engagement story that would last a lifetime.

1. What are some of your favorite engagement stories?

***Read aloud Ruth 3***

2. Look more carefully at verses 1-6. Describe Naomi's plan and her motives.

3. In what ways did Ruth and Naomi show consideration for the feelings and reputation of Boaz?

4. If an elderly man today woke up and found a young woman sleeping at the foot of his bed, what do you think he would do?

How was Boaz's response the same — or different from — what
you would expect?



5. If Boaz had taken sexual advantage of Ruth, probably no one
   else would have known. In your own life, what situations create
   opportunity for you to act out of integrity?



6. In verse 9, Ruth asked Boaz to "spread the corner of your
   garment over me," a symbol of commitment. What all was she
   saying about herself in that verse?



7. In verse 10, Boaz said that Ruth was kind. Why?



8. In what ways did Boaz show his own kindness?



9. What plans did they make for the morning?



10. In most engagements today, one person says, "Will you . . . ?"
    and the other says, "I will . . ." What did Ruth and Boaz say to
    each other that accomplished the same thing?

11. Several times in this story Ruth, Boaz, and Naomi speak of God. Review each of these references to God so far in the Book of Ruth. In view of these statements, how would you describe the relationship between their lives and their faith?

12. Take stock of the ways you do (or do not) use God's name. What do your words imply about your faith?

13. Study verses 16-18. How do you picture Ruth's arrival in the morning?

14. Ruth's potential remarriage might have been a threat to Naomi. What character qualities in each person in the story caused her not to feel threatened?

15. As the story of Ruth unfolds, we can begin to see God's kindness at work—perhaps in ways that Ruth and Naomi could not see at the time. How has hindsight shown you God's kindness in your own life? (Consider career choices, marriage, family, schools, places you have lived, etc.)

## Continuing with Worship

### God Is So Good

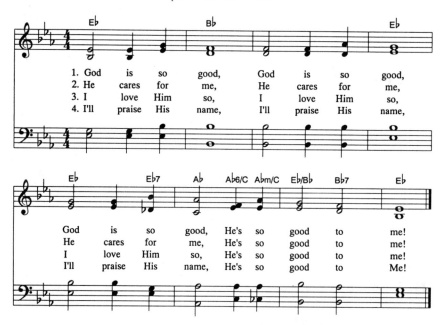

TEXT and MUSIC: Traditional

GOD IS SO GOOD
Irregular meter

## Continuing with Prayer

✦ Thank God for particular events in your life that you see as signs of His kindness to you.

✦ Mention to God the names of people who have shown you kindness in one way or another. Thank Him for them.

✦ Search your mind for opportunities that you have for showing kindness, or for people who need your kindness. Talk to God about these people and situations. Ask Him to show you ways to extend kindness to them.

## Kindness

*Just the corner of your garment*
*is enough to show your claim.*
*But I am cold*
*and so's the wind,*
*so cold.*

*A crucifix*
*hung high*
*against dark sky*

*And I*
*wrapped warm*
*in seamless garment*
*shed for me.*

−CN

# 8
# Faithful Friends

*Ruth 4*

I don't keep a prayer list. Actually, I do keep a notebook divided by days so that over the course of a week I worship God in a variety of ways and pray for a variety of people and events. But I don't keep a list that says "requests made/date answered." I have godly friends, whom I respect, who keep this kind of list—and perhaps some day I shall also. These friends tell me that their dated prayer list is a great encouragement to their faith. With it they see God at work through their prayers; they remind themselves that what once worried them intensely, God in His kindness has now resolved, and they use it as an outline for thanksgiving.

But there's something about putting God on a dated checklist that makes me feel a bit presumptuous. What if my life's circumstances are rotten, and my prayers go unanswered? Furthermore, what if, when I pray, I feel like I'm talking to the wall? Or worse, to myself. What do I do with my prayer checklist on weeks like that? Do I give God a D minus?

When Naomi returned with Ruth to her Bethlehem home, she said, "The Almighty has made my life very bitter." While she may have blamed God for circumstances that would be bitter for any of us, she at least acknowledged God's presence in her life. That, in itself, was an act of faith. She did not assume that God had looked away for a while and had forgotten to answer her prayers. To walk with God, even in the bitter times, takes great faith indeed.

Naomi's story has a happy ending—and it ends, appropriately, with praise to God. Will my own story (so similar to Naomi's) end in a similar way? I cannot say. But I want to believe that God is faithful, and to praise Him anyway—no matter how my story ends. God is not a friend just for the end of the story when the story comes out well. He is a friend for the journey.

1. Name one friend who has nourished your faith. How and under what circumstances has that person helped you to grow?

***Read aloud Ruth 4:1-12***

2. What all can you know from this text about the business and social customs of Bethlehem?

3. What steps did Boaz take to make a fair and public transaction?

4. Boaz began his transaction in verse 1 by calling his rival kinsman-redeemer, "my friend." In what ways did the elders act as *friends* to both parties?

5. Why do you think that the kinsman-redeemer first said that he would buy Naomi's land and later said that he would not?

6. Notice the blessing these witnesses and friends gave to Boaz in verses 11-12. Of what purpose is the mention of characters from his family tree? (Hint: Take a quick look at Genesis 38.)

7. Make a mental survey of your own family tree — even its unsavory members. What character qualities do you see (perhaps even in one of its less successful members) that you would like to develop in yourself — and maybe even pass on to someone else?

8. The friends of Boaz encouraged him by reminding him of God's work in past generations of his family. How have you seen God at work in the past generations of your own family?

### *Read aloud Ruth 4:13-22*

9. You began your study of this book by creating a mental portrait of Naomi as she appeared in the opening paragraphs. How would you paint her portrait in this closing section? (Consider colors, technique, other people, mood, what you would want your viewer to feel.)

10. In what ways did Naomi's friends encourage her — and encourage her faith?

11. Notice the words of Naomi's friends in verse 17, "Naomi has a son." What did this mean to the various people in the story — Ruth, Boaz, Naomi, the people of Bethlehem?

12. Even though Naomi had experienced great tragedy in her past, her friends encouraged her at this point to praise God. What do you think of the timing of their invitation to join them in praising God?

13. How could you begin to acknowledge God's faithful presence in your life — even when circumstances are not to your liking?

14. Bring to mind at least one person among your own circle of friends who could use your encouragement at this time. What could you do or say that might encourage him or her?

# Continuing with Worship

## Great Is Thy Faithfulness

1. Great is Thy faith-ful-ness, O God my Fa-ther, There is no sha-dow of
2. Sum-mer and win-ter, and spring-time and har-vest, Sun, moon, and stars in their
3. Par-don for sin and a peace that en-dur-eth, Thy own dear pres-ence to

turn-ing with Thee; Thou chang-est not, Thy com-pas-sions they fail not; As Thou hast
cours-es a-bove Join with all na-ture in man-i-fold wit-ness To Thy great
cheer and to guide; Strength for to-day and bright hope for to-mor-row, Bles-sings all

been Thou for-e-ver wilt be.
faith-ful-ness, mer-cy and love. Great is Thy faith-ful-ness! Great is Thy faith-ful-ness!
mine, with ten thou-sand be-side!

Morn-ing by morn-ing new mer-cies I see; All I have need-ed Thy

hand hath pro - vid-ed.   Great is Thy faith - ful - ness, Lord, un - to   me!    A - men.

Thomas O. Chisholm (1866-1960)                        FAITHFULNESS 11 10 11 10 w/refrain
                                                      William M. Runyan (1870-1957)

## Continuing with Prayer

✦ Express in your own words your thanks to God that He is your faithful friend.

✦ Consider some of the major turning points in your life. Thank God for the ways that you can now see His work in your life at that time.

✦ What current circumstances make it difficult for you to believe that God is exercising kindness toward you? Express your feelings to God about this situation, then ask Him to give your faith endurance in spite of these circumstances.

✦ Who needs your faithful friendship? Spend a few moments in silence asking God to bring an appropriate person to mind. Then pray for that person and for your role in his or her life.

## Naomi's Son

*He pats*
*the worn and wrinkled face*
*that sings a lullaby*
*learned ages back*
*for babies never born.*

*She praises God*
*and laughs.*

—CN

# Notes for Leaders

## Preparation

**Begin your preparation with prayer and personal study.** Prepare to lead your particular lesson by following the ten steps under *Suggestions for Personal Study* beginning on page 8.

**Study the biblical context of the passage under consideration.** Research any questions likely to sidetrack your group.

**Study the flow of questions.** TruthSeed questions are designed to create a flow of discussion from beginning to end. Get comfortable with the potential directions of the study. Mark pacing notes so that the discussion will spread evenly over your allotted time. Most TruthSeed studies should last about an hour.

**Read the leader's notes for your particular study** beginning on page 000. Mark information that you may need during the course of the study in the blank spaces of your question list.

**If your group time includes other ingredients such as refreshments, music, worship, sharing, and prayer, plan time divisions** so that your group is able to accomplish all that is scheduled. Many TruthSeed lessons make suggestions for these additional ingredients at the close of the Bible study section.

**Acknowledge to yourself and to God that the group belongs to the people in it, not to you as a leader.** TruthSeed is designed to facilitate a group discovery form of learning moderated by a discussion leader. Plan to lead with the group's welfare and interests in mind.

**Pray for each group member by name.**

# Group Time

**Begin on time.** No apology necessary. The group has come together for a particular purpose and has assigned you the job of leading it in the study.

**If your group is meeting for the first time, survey together the guidelines** for group discussion on page 7. This will help each person to know what is expected and will get you off on a common footing.

**Take appropriate note of the narrative introduction at the beginning of the study then ask the opening question.** Encourage responses from each person. When everyone seems involved in the subject at hand, the group will be ready to enter the biblical text. Since the opening questions point toward the text but do not interact with it, always ask the opening question BEFORE reading the Scripture.

**Read the assigned Scripture passage aloud.** Or ask several group members to read. Some people feel embarrassed about their reading skills, so don't make surprise assignments unless you are certain that they will be well accepted. Paragraph breaks in the text mark natural thought divisions, so always read by paragraphs, not by verses.

**Conduct a discussion of the biblical text using the questions supplied.** TruthSeed questions should promote multiple answers and group interaction. Allow time for several people to respond to each question and to each other. If the group does not seem to understand a particular question, rephrase it until it becomes clear, break it into smaller units, or give a brief summary and move on.

**Give encouraging comments.** If an answer is partially right, acknowledge that part. If an answer seems inappropriate, say something like, "What verse led you to that conclusion?" or "What do some of the rest of you think?"

**Don't be afraid of silence.** Help group members to become comfortable with the quiet by announcing a "thinking time." Then invite them to share their thoughtful responses to the questions at hand. Learn a sensitivity to God that can come from occasional silence.

**Pace the study.** It is the leader's responsibility to be sure that you finish on time and that the group has adequate time to discuss later questions. Some questions will take longer than others, so create a flexible pace with one eye on the clock and the other on interests of your group. Don't be afraid to redirect attention to the question list or the biblical text. Suggest that you may come back to some interesting topic after you have finished the study.

**Involve everyone—more or less equally.** Draw in quiet people by asking for nonthreatening opinion responses. Avoid direct eye contact with someone who talks a bit too much. If necessary, point out the shared responsibility for a successful discussion by reading item 4 on page 7.

**Avoid over-talking yourself.** Groups with an overactive leader get tempted to sit back and let the leader do *all* the work. Eventually, this causes people to lose the benefit of a personal encounter with the Scripture as it impacts their own lives.

**Keep the discussion on track.** Consider writing the purpose statement from the leader's section at the top of your question page so that you can keep the discussion objective in mind. You can head off a tangent by gently directing attention back to the biblical text. But do consider the relative merit of any potential tangent. Sometimes apparent tangents represent real needs that the group ought to address. In that case, adjust your plan (for the moment) and follow the needs of the group. If the tangent seems of limited interest or importance, offer to talk about it in more detail at a later time. Or if the tangent is of great importance, but requires further preparation, ask the group to table it for this session, but come back to it at a later meeting.

**Don't skip questions of personal application.** Here is where Scripture does its most important work. As other group members respond, be ready to add your own experiences of God's work in your life.

**Open and close your study with prayer.** Or ask someone in your group to do so.

# Study One
## Wrong Ways and U-Turns
### *Jonah 1*

*Purpose: To appreciate God's intervention in our lives when we have made wrong turns.*

**Question 1.** Try to involve each person in your group with this question. Accept each person's contribution with grace. This is a time for sharing history, not for judging the merits of what contributes to each other's contentment.

**Question 2.** Some may feel that their most contented point is now, that it has not yet closed. Others will have been through the traumatic end of an era that they can never reclaim. Hear these stories with gentle acceptance. Encourage brevity, so that your group can begin its study of the text. The purpose here is to establish some empathy for Jonah who was about to see his own age of contentment come to a crashing end.

**Question 4.** Help your group to trace the actions, mood, storm, and conversation throughout verses 1-9. People should should note that the main characters are God, Jonah, the captain, and the sailors. Encourage the group to examine the minutia of the text and throw in a dash of creativity as they express how they would capture these events in sound and film. As a point of information, you might mention that the sailors were probably the famous Phoenicians of the Iron Age, that Joppa is the modern seaport of Jaffa, and that Tarshish was probably located in Spain. Pottery inscriptions indicate that Phoenician trade routes took ships to Spain—the outer reaches of then-known geography. Jonah was headed as far away from God's assignment as he could get.

**Question 5.** Your group should discuss the implied beliefs of the captain in verse 6, the sailors in verses 5, 7-8, the writer of the story in verses 1-2, 4, and Jonah in verses 3, 9. This is an important question because one of the major impacts of the storm was that everybody changed their beliefs about God. It is therefore important to see the belief system with which each character entered the story.

**Question 6.** Compare what Jonah says about God in verse 9 with his various actions thus far in the story.

**Question 7.** Each of us has times when we do not quite live up to our beliefs. If your group members have not yet built much trust in each other, people may hesitate to speak here, since this question requires some admission of shortcomings. Be ready with a couple of fairly nonthreatening examples from your own experience, then encourage several others to respond in similar manner. You can encourage them by a reminder that one of the first steps to growth is to know where we are weak.

**Question 8.** Your group should cite information in verses 4, 5, 10-11, and 13. It might help to note that these frightened sailors were probably Phoenician—the most skillful seamen of their time.

**Question 10.** Various examples of selfishness and selflessness occur in verses 11-15.

**Question 11.** Compare the actions of the sailors in verses 14 and 16 with their original view expressed in verse 5. If you would like a follow-up question at this point, ask: *Do you think the sailors saw the fish? If so, how do you think that would affect their view of Jonah's God?*

**Question 12.** For some people, Jonah's "whale" is the number one reason why they cannot believe what the Bible says is true. They know all about gastric juices and human need for oxygen and comparative size of people and fish guts. They say: *It can't happen, therefore it didn't happen, therefore I can't rely on any factual information in Scripture.* It's unlikely that you can solve this kind of dilemma in the course of your brief study. But several options are open.

First, it is possible for people to study a text together even if not everyone agrees about the factual reliability of the text. Even if the Jonah account *is* just a "story," it is a story told to illustrate a point. So if people disagree about the nature of the story, they can still go on to talk about its meaning.

Second, verse 17 does not call this sea creature a *whale*. It says instead, "The LORD provided a great fish." It is possible that this fish was a miracle, a special creation by God, fully equipped to nurture Jonah for three days.

Jonah's faith statement in verse 9 holds this as a possibility. "The God of heaven, who made the sea and the land," could have also created a special fish to show up at just the right moment in the storm that He also created.

If your group has varying beliefs about the veracity of this story, now is probably not the time to stage a war about miracles and special fish and verbal inspiration of Scripture. Instead, just let the group ponder the comparison of verses 9 and 17. Acknowledge that you can all agree that this story (true or not) does illustrate some important truths, and move on (together) from there.

**Questions 13, 14.** Encourage a more personal level of sharing here than was possible in previous application questions. Rather than one or two long stories, try to gather several shorter ones. Give each person present an opportunity to make some response. If the shortened versions of the stories imply a longer version that you sense ought to be told, make time after the study or during the week to hear its enlarged version.

**Continuing.** If your group has additional time together after the Bible study section of your meeting, use the music as a time of worship. You can guide your group to comment on what this hymn, written by William Cowper, reveals about Jonah's God (and ours) and what encouragement we can find in his words. Then use the prayer suggestions for guided silent or voiced prayers.

Your group may take interest in some background information about William Cowper. He lived from 1731 to 1800 and struggled all his life with bouts of depression and near madness. His mental instability made it almost impossible for him to fully believe that God loved him. Even so, he was able to write the kind of faith statement appearing in this hymn. If your group does not sing, try reading the words as a poem.

# Study Two
## Journey to the Bottom
### *Jonah 2*

*Purpose: To increase our commitment to God by taking time to communicate honestly with Him — even in our times of despair.*

**Question 1.** Take as much time as necessary to explore this two-part question. Use it to allow group members to get acquainted with the spiritual issues that each one faces. Some may see spending prolonged time alone with God as a frightening proposition. (Jonah probably did.) They can discuss how they would use the time: sleep, read a novel, count the hours with hash marks on the wall. Others might welcome the opportunity. They too can mention how they would use the time and what issues they would likely take up in prayer and study.

**Question 2.** Use this question to survey the passage. Your group should point out the following phrases: *distress* (v. 2), *depths of the grave* (v. 2), *called for help* (v. 2), *into the deep* (v. 3), *very heart of the seas* (v. 3), *currents swirled about me* (v. 3), *waves and breakers swept over me* (v. 3), *engulfing waters* (v. 5), *deep surrounded me* (v. 5), *seaweed was wrapped around my head* (v. 5), *roots of the mountains* (v. 6), *sank down* (v. 6), *the pit* (v. 6), *my life was ebbing away* (v. 7). Some may point out that even though the whole chapter is a prayer to God, it is not until verse 3 that Jonah begins to address God directly.

**Question 3.** Your group may have a variety of guesses. Jonah may have envied this sea creature so at home in a sea that was deadly to himself. He may have felt even more frightened of the fish than he was of the sea. Or he may have seen the fish as a potential instrument of rescue from drowning. Regardless of his initial feelings, verses 2-7 reveal as graphic description of drowning as we are likely to find in literature. By verse 7, without divine intervention, Jonah is seconds from death.

**Note:** If your group still has questions regarding whether this is a true story with a real fish, review the suggestions for handling this issue in the leader's notes of lesson 1, question 12.

**Question 4.** Your group should notice particularly the words *cling, worthless, forfeit,* and *grace.* Use these questions to help people interpret some of Jonah's new perspective on his mission. Was Jonah's flight to "freedom" a pursuit after one of his own idols? Is he now admitting that freedom from God's command is worthless? Is he hoping for the grace of God's forgiveness — and perhaps a second chance at his assignment? Regarding Nineveh, were the people there idol worshipers? Is Jonah now admitting that God's grace could even extend to these people who are the enemies of his nation? As your group members discuss the two questions of number 4, they may come to some conclusions regarding Jonah's idols and God's grace.

**Question 6.** Jonah's references to God appear in verses 1-2, 4, 6-7, 9. Help your group to study each one and discuss appropriate conclusions. If you want an optional question at this point, ask: *What do these statements, taken in sequence, say about the progress of Jonah's relationship with God?*

**Question 7.** Pause long enough here for several people to suggest ways or times that their praying has mirrored Jonah's. Encourage them to be as specific as possible. As a few brief stories are shared, your group members will become more aware of each other's hardships — and what others in the group have learned through their experiences. Encourage honest communication by not assuming that all of these stories will have a happily-ever-after ending. Be ready with an account of one of your own "belly of the fish" prayers.

**Question 8.** Jonah made three major statements of faith in this book — not that he constantly lived up to those statements any better than we do. His first faith statement appears in Jonah 1:9; his second one in 2:8-9. Help your group to discuss the spiritual progress reflected by these two statements. The group should also compare Jonah's actions and intended actions at this point with those in the early part of the story. In 1:9, Jonah is still running from God — though he is about to ask the sailors to throw him out of the ship. His words at the end of chapter 2, however, suggest that he recognizes idolatry in himself, that he is ready to abandon those idols, that he is thanking God and willing to sacrifice to Him, that he will make good on his vows (perhaps the vows of a prophet).

**Question 9.** What did Jonah mean by his statement about salvation? Jonah could not have known the full theological meaning of personal salvation that is attached to Christ's life, death, and resurrection. Yet, Jonah's experience in the sea gave him an intuitive understanding of the salvation concept. Did he mean that God saved him from the sea? That he trusted God to save him from the fish? That God would preserve his physical life? Or was he thinking of spiritual salvation? His own? Nineveh's? Your group may suggest these or other possible meanings to Jonah's statement.

**Question 10.** Use this question to help your group make the jump from Jonah's era to your own. For us, with New Testament hindsight, salvation has a deeper meaning. Encourage various group members to express in simple language, free of Christian clichés, what they would mean if they were to make this statement to a friend. Encourage explanations that reflect their own stories— much as they have witnessed Jonah telling his.

**Question 11.** Your group may express a variety of explanations for the fish. Was the fish Jonah's submarine trip back to land? (The text does not tell us where Jonah landed so unceremoniously. But we may guess that it was nearer to Nineveh than to Tarshish.) Was the purpose of the fish to allow Jonah forced time alone with God? Was the fish an opportunity for Jonah to see what God's salvation meant to him—and therefore to the people of Nineveh? Was the purpose of the fish to help Jonah see that he could not escape God? Was the fish experiential evidence of God's power and of His personal concern that Jonah obey him? The text does not explain *why* God provided this special fish. In view of the text thus far, let your group suggest these or other answers.

**Question 12.** Use this question to provide a time of thoughtful self-examination. First read aloud the options for self examination, then allow several minutes of prayerful silence. Encourage each person to select one of the areas and make some notes in the space provided. After this period of quiet, ask if any are willing to talk about what they have written. If your group has a follow-up period of worship and prayer, you may refer back to this question during that time.

**Continuing.** Ask your group to read through the text of this hymn and mention themes that echo their discussion of Jonah 2. If the group enjoys singing, sing this hymn of commitment together. If not, read it aloud to each other. Follow your time of music by using the prayer suggestions for guided silent or voiced prayers.

# Study 3
## Second Chances
### *Jonah 3*

*Purpose: To appreciate God's compassion in the second chances that He has given us and to extend similar compassion to others.*

**Question 1.** Encourage each person who is willing to mention at least one second chance incident. It can be as minor as being given a warning instead of a traffic ticket, or as major as recovery from a life-threatening illness. Be sure that some people talk about what they did with that second chance. Some will have built on the opportunity to bring about improvement. Others will admit that even with a second chance they simply made a similar mistake again. The purpose of the discussion is to help group members get to know each others' histories and to identify with Jonah—his second chance and what he did with it.

**Question 2.** Your group should pick out similar phrases in the first two verses of Jonah 1 and Jonah 3. As for why the story is told in this way, the repetition of God's command highlights Jonah's second opportunity. It also gives Jonah a chance to demonstrate any lasting change that occurred inside the fish.

**Question 3.** Help group members to look for signs of repentance in Jonah, in the Ninevites, even (perhaps) in God. They should find something in almost every verse. If a question comes up regarding whether God repented (a term used by KJV and RSV in verse 10), suggest that you will discuss that problem more fully later in the study. Your group will at least notice that God did not immediately bring the judgment on Nineveh that Jonah had announced. Discussion of question 3 should form a background of information for the remainder of the study.

**Question 4.** Your group should point out such verbs as *obeyed, went, started, proclaimed.* Members should then discuss any internal changes that had to take place in Jonah in order for him to do these actions—compared to his actions in chapter one. Why did he make this change? Because he was convinced that God gave him no real choice? Because he now agreed with God's plan? Because he wanted to proclaim this kind of message to his enemies? Because he no longer feared for his life? (If an ocean and a fish hadn't done him in, why fear a mere city full of enemies?) Or maybe Jonah never did care much about living—and still didn't. (This would explain why he so quickly suggested, in chapter 1, that the sailors throw him overboard.) We can't know all of Jonah's motives, but a discussion of what they might have been could prove interesting. Some people may suggest that you examine his motives in view of chapter 4. If so, point out that the events of chapter 4 occurred at a later time. So in fairness to the story, let's take Jonah's actions in chapter 3 at face value at that point in the series of events.

If you want an additional question at this point say: *Jonah had to travel some 500 miles (which took as long as a month) to get to Nineveh. What do you think he said to God during the trip? Why didn't he turn back at some point?*

**Note:** Some question exists about the size of Nineveh. If the events of this book occurred in the first half of the 8th century B.C., Nineveh was in decline at that time and hardly demanded three days to traverse. The time—"three days"—could describe the time necessary to visit "Greater Nineveh" which included Rehoboth Ir, Calah, and Resen (*NIV Study Bible,* p. 1368). The three days might also refer to the time it took to walk and preach in each street. Or it might assume the first day as an arrival day, the second as a preaching day, and the third as departure. In any event, it's hard to overlook the parallel to Jonah's three days in the fish.

In a related issue, we may also ask: *How can Scripture describe a city barely a mile across as a "great city"?* (v. 2) In *Tyndale Old Testament Commentaries*, Alexander, Baker, and Waltke respond that a proper translation of Nineveh's description in verses 2-3 is "a great city to God," an interpretation confirmed by the closing events of the story.

**Question 5.** Encourage several to respond with personal accounts. Your discussion of the second part of the question should point out that obedience (for any motive) is better than disobedience. But their experiences will probably illustrate that reluctant obedience results in inner turmoil. It may also cause inability to "see" or "buy into" God's larger design. Discussion of this question will prepare the group to better understand and empathize with Jonah's actions in the book's final chapter.

**Question 6.** Your group may have covered the gist of this question when it responded to question 3. If so, you can briefly review the signs of repentance, then focus on the more far-reaching effects. If your group needs a breakdown into smaller questions, ask: *How would the king's behavior affect them? How would the condition of their animals affect them? What impact would the king's words have?*

**Note:** Regarding sackcloth and ashes, "The sackcloth used was a thick coarse cloth, normally made from goat's hair; to wear it symbolized the rejection of earthly comforts and pleasures. . . . The King sits on the ground amid dust or ashes. In so doing he symbolizes his human frailty and worthlessness" (*Obadiah, Jonah, Micah*, Desmond Alexander, David W. Baker, and Bruce Waltke. *Tyndale Old Testament Commentaries*, D.J. Wiseman, General Editor. p. 122).

**Question 7.** Your group should cite such words in the text as *wickedness* (1:2), *evil ways* (3:8, 10), and *violence* (3:8). The fact that they were all to *call urgently on God* (3:8) suggests that this was not their normal pattern of worship, that they may have worshiped other gods. The phrase *Nineveh will be overturned* (3:4) suggests that Nineveh (capital city of Assyria) may have been an oppressor nation, a description which history confirms.

**Question 8.** In order to respond in the way they did, the people of Nineveh would have reached several conclusions about God: that He opposes evil, that He punishes violence, that He is powerful enough to destroy them, that He listens to prayer, that He could see them, that He wanted them to change, that He had sent Jonah, that He might give them a second chance. Your group should mention these or similar concepts.

**Question 9.** If you need to divide this question into smaller units, ask: *What are appropriate ways for people who believe in God to show repentance? How do people who do not believe in God repent? How do new believers repent?*

**Question 13.** Scripture teaches that one of God's attributes is immutability. God does not change. (See Numbers 23:19-20 and Malachi 3:6, for examples.) *Why then did God instruct Jonah to prophesy destruction, then turn back on His promise? Was God toying with Jonah? Was God governed by the actions of the repenting people?* Let your group members discuss these questions for a few moments. They will probably come to conclusions similar to those explained in the *NIV Study Bible:* "The Lord retains the right of limiting His own absolute sovereignty on the basis of human response to His offers of pardon and restoration and His threats of judgment and destruction. *If . . . if . . . if . . . if.* God's promises and threats are conditioned on man's actions. God who Himself does not change . . . nevertheless will change His preannounced response to man, depending on what the latter does" (p. 1152).

**Questions 14, 15.** Pace the study so that you allow time for thoughtful personal answers here. Encourage everyone present to respond in some way. Be ready to enter this phase of the discussion, not as a leader, but with the vulnerability of a fellow member of the group.

**Continuing.** Sing the simple worship song several times. If your group members are experienced singers, try singing in two-part antiphony. Then lead the group in prayer using the outline suggested.

# Study 4
## The Uncontrollably Compassionate God
### *Jonah 4*

*Purpose: To appreciate God's compassion for those who do not deserve His grace — ourselves included.*

**Question 1.** Aim for brief but personal responses from each person.

**Question 2.** Use this question to help your group survey the passage. Potentially surprising events occur in 3:10; 4:2-3, 5, 7, and 11.

**Question 3.** See the details of verse 2. People in your group may disagree about whether or not Jonah was telling the truth. They may cite his behavior in the previous three chapters to defend one point of view or the other. Jonah's honesty (or lack of it) with God is interesting, but not necessarily significant to the story's main concepts.

**Question 4.** Your group should notice all five qualities of God that Jonah mentions in verse 2.

**Question 5.** Encourage people to express some honest reflection on their own character so that they can better appreciate the character of God. You can set an example by mentioning some of your own specific actions or traits that cause you to be grateful for God's compassion.

**Question 6.** You might remind your group of the 40 days mentioned in Jonah 3:4. Was Jonah planning to wait out the entire time? Or had he waited that long already? Was he gloating? Why wasn't he mixing with the newly repentant and converted people of Nineveh? Was he afraid that he would die with them? Did he fear them? Was he thinking that if he sulked long enough God would change His mind again? Let your group discuss these or other motives.

**Question 8.** Allow people in your group to make a brief review of these verses and then express their own conclusions about Jonah's state of mind. Was he seriously depressed? Desperate? Or was he merely blustering? Would his lack of respect for his own life influence how he felt about the people of Nineveh?

**Question 11.** Let people in your group first answer spontaneously—as though they were in Jonah's shoes. Then help them to focus on the word *right*. As they do so, they will have to consider Jonah's position as it relates to God's authority. We have all kinds of *rights* when we relate to other people, but few (if any) when we relate to God—except the right to be called His child.

**Question 12.** This acted-out parable may seem, at first, confusing to some people in your group. They may wonder if God is torturing Jonah. As they discuss the question they may notice some similarities between the vine and Nineveh. They may also notice some difference in Jonah's feelings for Nineveh and his feelings for the vine—and discuss why he viewed them differently. Finally, they may notice some differences between Jonah's interests and God's concern for the people and even the animals of Nineveh. Allow your group to study the events in verses 5-11 in order to figure out God's purposes in these events. Discussion of this question should lead naturally into question 13.

**Question 13.** Be sure that your group treats all three subjects of Jonah's education: God, Nineveh, and himself. People should notice that God is compassionate to the inhabitants of Nineveh, even to the cattle. They should notice that the people of Nineveh are ignorant (verse 11 says that they *cannot tell their right hand from their left*). This probably refers to their ignorance of God's moral law. And if Jonah is so angry at the people that he cannot care about them, God mentions their animals—who certainly deserved no suffering. As for himself, Jonah had opportunity to see his own selfishness—that he cared about the vine only because it shaded him. The vine did not belong to him; God created it—along with the east wind. The people of Nineveh did not belong to Jonah either, even though God had assigned him as their missionary. But Nineveh *and* Jonah were subject to God's wrath *and* His mercy.

**Question 14.** Encourage each person to respond in some way. They should feel free to draw from any part of the book.

**Question 15.** Use this closing question to lead into your time of worship and prayer.

**Note:** *What happened after the end of this story?* The book of Jonah ends with the main character brooding outside the newly redeemed city and complaining to God that he wants to die. We do not know what happened to Jonah—whether he ever fully received God's acted-out message of compassion. But other parts of Scripture and secular history tell us what happened to Nineveh. If year estimates are correct, Jonah visited Nineveh in the 760s B.C. We can assume that Nineveh's repentance lasted for some time because we don't hear any more about Nineveh until 723–722. (Remember, we're going backward in years.) At that time, if Jonah was still alive, his worst fears were realized. Brutal soldiers from Nineveh swept through his country of Israel. They deported his people, scattered them throughout their other conquered nations, and brought strangers to resettle the land. These ten tribes of Israel were so thoroughly erased that they became the legendary "ten lost tribes of Israel."

But God was still not finished with Nineveh. In 612 B.C., 150 years later, the destruction that God had threatened through Jonah came upon Nineveh. This time God used an alliance of the Babylonians, Medes, and Scythians to conquer this once-powerful capital city of Assyria. The Old Testament prophet Nahum, probably writing just prior to Nineveh's downfall, took up Jonah's job of warning the people of Nineveh. This time, biblical readers see no repentance— from Nineveh or from God. With that, history ushered in a new era with a new world power: the Babylonians.

What can we conclude from Jonah's ministry and God's compassion? The Apostle Paul writing to the church at Rome summarizes it well: "What then shall we say? Is God unjust? Not at all! For He says to Moses, 'I will have mercy on whom I have mercy, and I will have compassion on whom I have compassion'" (Romans 9:14-15). Those of us who are God's people can echo, even with mystified raised eyebrows, "So be it."

**Continuing.** Use the printed music to sing (or read) your worship of God. Then use the suggestions provided to lead guided prayer.

# Study Five
## Loving and Letting Go
### *Ruth 1*

*Purpose: To hold on to faith in God even when we must love the people closest to us by letting them let go.*

**Question 1.** In-laws are often the butt of family jokes, sometimes undeservedly. Use this question to prompt some stories appreciative of in-laws. (Almost everyone should have at least one in-law related to them that they can say something good about.) If some of these stories generate sparks of humor, all the better. If the group seems sobered by the chapter introduction, give a few moments of time for people to absorb and comment on its impact, then introduce this first question.

**Question 2.** Encourage thoughtful visual images with this question. If people seem to need follow-up questions ask: *What would you use as background? What colors would you use? Black and white? What materials? Paints? Photography? What mood would you try to capture? What angle or pose? What would you want people to think or feel when they studied the portrait? What picture do you see when you think of Naomi?*

**Question 3.** Your group should find information in verses 1, 3, and 5, as well as note that Naomi and her daughters-in-law were all childless at this point.

**Question 4.** Your group should point out the information in verses 2, 4, 6-7. Consult a map to discover the distance and terrain over which the journey to and from Moab took place. Notice also the ten years mentioned in verse 4. Were both Ruth and Orpah infertile during that time? Or were they married late in that period? In view of the text, infertility is certainly possible—and a contributing disaster. For your own background information on the testy relationship between Israel and Moab, see Numbers 22:4–24:25, Deuteronomy 23:3-6, and Judges 3:12-30. You can then convey to your group any information that you find there that seems important. Rather than interrupt the discussion of Ruth 1 at this point, you can then refer them to these texts for further study on their own time.

**Question 5.** Most families have not faced the kind devastation that Naomi saw, yet most people have had moments when they could have felt similar disillusion with God. Create an opportunity for people to speak of those times and the feelings that came with them.

**Question 6.** Be sure your group deals with both parts of the question.

**Question 7.** Use all of verses 6-15. If you need a follow-up question try: *How do Naomi's words in verses 11-13 highlight her loss?* Your group should notice that even though Naomi loved her daughters-in-law so much that they kissed and wept at parting, she loved them enough to let them go. She cared more about their future than her own loneliness.

**Question 10.** Help your group to study, phrase by phrase, the intense commitment of verses 16-17.

**Question 12.** Encourage people in your group to walk Naomi's homecoming with her as they talk through the details of each verse.

**Question 13.** Study Naomi's references to God in verses 8-9, 13, 20-21, and discuss the concepts of God that they reflect. If you need follow-up questions to get the discussion going, try: *What is God like, according to Naomi? What is His nature, His character, His purpose?*

**Question 14.** Your group should enter into Naomi's dilemma as best it can. People can respond to this question by using their own biblical knowledge or their personal experience with God. If you wish, try dividing the group into pairs. Ask one person to play the role of Naomi and the other to encourage and comfort her. Then reconvene the group for a closing time of worship and prayer.

**Continuing.** Use the music and prayer suggestions to move your group from study to worship.

# Study 6

## Quiet Commitment

### *Ruth 2*

*Purpose: To worship God in the small behaviors of our lives in spite of the violent forces around us.*

**Question 1.** Encourage each person to participate in some way.

**Question 2.** Your group can find information about Boaz (either stated or implied) in verses 1, 3, 4-5, 8-9, 11-12, 14-16, and 20.

**Question 3.** Find information in verses 8-10, 22.

**Question 4.** These passages may seem confusing to people in your group, but they form a basis for the rest of the book, so try to help people understand the levirate laws. The gist of them is that the brother of a widow's husband was responsible to provide the widow with an heir and to redeem her property — property that she might have sold or mortgaged. Most men (understandably) declined this responsibility.

This law, which may seem unfeeling compared to today's ideals of romantic love, was actually a practical protection to widowed women. Through it, vulnerable women could retain both family and property. Ruth's situation did not exactly fit the pattern of Deuteronomy 25, which assumes that the widow is still capable of bearing children and that her dead husband had a living brother. The biblical text, however, mentions no brother for Elimelech (Naomi's dead husband), and Ruth 1:11-13 assumes that Naomi is past menopause. If the law of levirate were to come into play in this story, Naomi would need a stand-in (Ruth), and some willing but distant male relative would have to fill the brother's position. Even so, Naomi evidently felt that she and Ruth could claim some of the protection of the levirate law — particularly if Elimelech's nearest male relative felt kindly toward them. And Boaz did.

**Question 5.** Your group examined the character of Boaz in question 2; this question turns attention to Ruth. Her character qualities are either stated or implied in verses 2-3, 7, 11, 13, 17-18, and 23. As your group talks through the text, suggest that people cite verse numbers so that everyone can track together the phrases and concepts that describe Ruth.

**Question 6.** Let your group study the various practices described in these verses and discuss the values that undergird those actions. By Ruth's era, some of the practices seem to have changed slightly, but the values remained—at least in the household of Boaz.

**Question 8.** Help your group to examine each phrase of verse 12. Follow-up questions might include: *What was Boaz saying about God when he spoke of repaying? When he spoke of rich reward? What did he mean when he said that God was the God of Israel? What do his words about wings and refuge suggest about God's nature?*

This might also be a good time to suggest that people look back at Ruth's commitment to Naomi (and Naomi's God) in Ruth 1:16. You could ask: *What impressions about her new religion might Ruth gain from Boaz' description here of his God?*

**Question 11.** Allow adequate time for people to recount their own stories here. Be prepared with one or two brief ones of your own. Try to make this a time when people do not play "Can you top this?" games with hardship stories. The adversity can be quite minor. Focus instead on God's kindness.

**Question 12.** If possible, help people to draw ideas from the story of Ruth. They might point out ways that they can keep old customs (and modify them) to suit current conditions, ways that they can bring God into their everyday speech and actions, ways that they can show kindness to each other in small ways, ways that they can care for poor people while at the same time providing opportunity for dignity, ways that they can make and keep commitments to each other, ways that they can honor and care for family members.

Once the group has mentioned several ideas based on the Ruth story thus far, you might have them expand the conversation to consider how they could live in more wholesome ways in spite of social pressures to the contrary.

**Continuing.** Use the music and prayer suggestions to provide an appropriate follow-up to your time of study.

# Study 7
## Counting Kindness
### *Ruth 3*

*Purpose: To reflect on God's kindness at work in our lives and to express that kindness in our relationships with other people.*

**Question 1.** Encourage all who are willing to participate in this question. Some may tell of their own engagement, others of a friend or family member. Humor will go a long way here. If possible, be ready with a humorous engagement story of your own.

**Question 2.** Help your group to focus first on verse 1 in order to define Naomi's motives. After that, people should study verses 2-6 to outline her plan. If questions arise about why she would have instructed her daughter-in-law to sneak into a strange man's bed in the middle of the night, you may refer to this quotation from the *NIV Study Bible:* "Although Naomi's instructions may appear forward, the moral integrity of Naomi and Ruth is never in doubt (see v. 11). Naomi's advice to Ruth is clearly for the purpose of appealing to Boaz's kinsman obligation. Ruth's actions were a request for marriage" (p. 368). If people wonder why a wealthy man like Boaz happened to be camping out during the harvest season, the same source suggests that this was common practice of a land owner just after harvest. He was protecting his produce from theft.

**Question 3.** Focus the attention of your group on verses 5-9. People should cite details throughout those verses that show consideration for Boaz and his reputation. If you wish to discuss additional questions at this point (and have the time for it) try: *How were Ruth's actions different from a prostitute's? Do you think that Ruth was trying to trick Boaz into something that he did not want to do? Explain.*

**Question 4.** Use the first question to help people see Boaz's dilemma—and his temptation. For the second half, help them to briefly survey the actions of Boaz throughout the rest of the chapter. They will study the actions in more detail later in this session.

**Question 5.** Help people to search their own circumstances for opportunities to exercise integrity—whether or not they have risen to the occasion. These need not be large moral issues. Integrity often is at its greatest test in the small details of our lives. Examples: the opportunity to report correct (or incorrect) time on a work time sheet, the chance to carry home office supplies, paying (or not paying) for personal photocopying at work, the choice in reading materials or TV or movie viewing when alone, the chance for an out-of-town friendship that might lead to an affair, what to do with incorrect change, inflating a complimentary story about ourselves, allowing other Christians to think that we are more "spiritual" than we really are, the opportunity to take advantage of someone who can't get back at us—and maybe wouldn't even know. Because Boaz had developed an inner integrity, he was able to act toward others (including Ruth) with genuine kindness. We can do the same.

**Question 6.** Help your group to focus on the details of verse 9. People should notice such words as *servant, corner, kinsman-redeemer*. Why did Ruth make such a request? Was she cold? If so, why just a corner of the garment? If people are confused about this symbol, use the following information from *NIV Study Bible:* "*Spread the corner of your garment over me.* A request for marriage. . . . A similar custom is still practiced in some parts of the Middle East today. There is a play on the words 'wings' of the Lord . . . and 'corners' . . . of the garment . . . both signifying protection. Boaz is vividly reminded that he must serve as the Lord's protective wing to watch over Ruth" (p. 368). As for "kinsman-redeemer," the same source says: "How Boaz was related to Ruth's former husband (Mahlon) is unknown, but the closest male relative had the primary responsibility to marry a widow. Naomi instructed Ruth to approach Boaz because he had already shown himself willing to be Ruth's protector. Boaz, however, would not bypass the directives of the law, which clearly gave priority to the nearest relative."

For further background information, read the Hebrew law on this subject in Deuteronomy 25:5-10. The levirate law described there is not exactly like the situation between Ruth and Boaz, but custom in the intervening years appears to have kept a similar form of this law. Leviticus 25:25 is also a factor.

If your group has already become familiar with these terms and customs, there is no need to review them at this point. But if details are fuzzy or if newcomers are present, a brief review might be in order.

**Questions 7–9.** Use these questions to study the details of verses 10-15. If your group has already covered the material when it discussed previous questions, move rather quickly through them, being sure that the group takes appropriate note of the couple's many ways of showing kindness to each other. If you need a clarifying question ask: *How was Ruth's action here a kindness to Boaz? To Naomi?* Since Boaz was related to Naomi, offspring between Ruth and Boaz could continue Naomi's genetic line. On an emotional level, Ruth's union with Boaz would not take Ruth away from Naomi, thus removing her one remaining family member. Instead, Ruth would add Boaz to the family fold.

**Question 10.** Let your group paraphrase the statements in verses 9 and 13.

**Question 11.** Treat each character separately. You will find references to God in Ruth 1:6, 8, 16, 20-21; 2:4, 12, 20; 3:10, 13.

**Question 13.** Help your group study verses 16-18 and paint visual and emotional images from the text.

**Question 14.** Use this question to let your group do a brief review of the book thus far and to trace some of the qualities of each character. You may find helpful information in 2:1, 11, 20, and 3:1, 8.

**Question 15.** Pace your study so that you give adequate time for reflection and discussion of this question. Be ready with a story or two from your own life (stories that are not too hard to top) and provide opportunity for others to relate examples of God's kindness in their own lives.

**Continuing.** Use the simple song here to remind yourselves of God's kindness and to praise Him for it. The tune is so easy that most groups can learn it in moments. Then use the suggestions for guided silent or spoken prayers. Or divide into pairs and use the prayer suggestions to pray together.

# Study 8
## Faithful Friends
### *Ruth 4*

*Purpose: To appreciate God's faithfulness and the faithfulness of our human friends.*

**Question 1.** Allow a minute or two for people to mentally survey their list of friends, then encourage each person to contribute a response. Help group members to be as specific as possible about the circumstances. If people seem to speak in generalities, ask: *Can you think of something specific that your friend did or said that helped you?* Or, *What character qualities of your friend helped you to develop in faith?*

**Question 2.** Your group should find information about customs throughout the passage. Examples: It seems that the place to conduct business was the town gate (v. 1). Elders were available there to assist with the transactions (v. 2). A kinsman-redeemer was a family relative who had certain property rights (at least first rights of refusal), but also had certain responsibilities (vv. 1, 4-7). A sandal passed from one person to the other seemed to be a symbol of a legal transaction (vv. 7-8). The elders served as witnesses to legal transactions (vv. 9-11). Use this question to survey the text. You will examine it in further detail as the study progresses.

**Question 3.** Use this question to help your group focus on Boaz and his words and actions. People should find a half dozen or so responses in the text.

**Question 4.** Let your group focus on the elders with this question. Notice that in verses 9-11, they are described three times as *witnesses*. This would assume that they were acting on behalf of both parties. Your group may notice that the elders were available for this service, not at home conducting their own affairs. Notice also the prayer of blessing they offered to Boaz at the end of the transaction.

**Question 5.** We can assume that the person with whom Boaz bargained did not at first realize that a marriage to Ruth was part of the bargain posed in verses 5-6. Perhaps he was already married. Maybe he did not want the added responsibility of a wife—and a mother-in-law. Maybe he worried that any future child would endanger the inheritance of his present children. Your group should study verses 2-6 and come up with these or similar conclusions.

**Question 6.** Genesis 38 shows that Perez was one of the twin boys born to Judah under somewhat scandalous circumstances. It seems that a woman named Tamar had married Judah's oldest son. The son died. According to the law of levirate described in Deuteronomy 25:5-6, the next son in line was to marry the widow and provide her with an heir. This would preserve her social and economic status in the community. Judah did allow his second son to marry Tamar, but he too died. By this time Judah understandably began to fear for the lives of his sons. So he refused to give the third son to Tamar.

Eventually, Tamar became pregnant, but no one knew the identity of the father. People complained to Judah that his daughter-in-law was guilty of prostitution. Judah made plans to execute Tamar under the death penalty. (Appropriate, in those days!) But Judah was in for one more surprise. It seemed that Tamar had concrete evidence that Judah himself was the father of her child. Twins, as it turned out. During Judah's recent trip to town, he had treated himself to a prostitute who remained veiled: Tamar. When confronted with that knowledge, Judah said, "She is more righteous than I," and he spared her life.

Perez was one of the resulting children, an ancestor of Boaz. So even though Judah's line was threatened with extinction, through

Tamar (and her son Perez) Judah became a great nation—the tribe where Boaz, Ruth, and Naomi lived.

Rachel and Leah were also famous ancestors, the wives of Jacob, father of the 12 tribes of Israel. Leah was Judah's mother (see Genesis 29:31-35). Ephrathah was the name for the area around Boaz's home town of Bethlehem. Your group may know much of this information, or be able to figure it out by a glance at Genesis 38. If not, give a brief summary, enough so that people can understand the blessing given in Ruth 4:11-12. Then move on with the study.

**Question 8.** Some people may feel hesitant to respond to this question, particularly if there are few people of faith in their family tree. Encourage them to look for ways that God may have used these people for the benefit of future generations, even though they themselves were not aware of it. God used even the rather sordid behavior of Judah and Tamar to create a lineage for the godly Boaz.

**Question 9.** People may want to recall the verbal portraits of Naomi that they created when they studied Ruth 1. While the book is named after Ruth, it is really Naomi's story. It is she who undergoes the change so highlighted by this beginning and ending description.

**Question 11.** Someone should point out that verses 18-22 look back several generations to Perez, the ancestor of Boaz, but they also look forward (through the union of Ruth and Boaz) to David, the most famous king in all of Hebrew history and the ancestor of Jesus Christ. (See Matthew 1:1.)

**Question 12.** If people are slow to respond, ask: *What would you think if the women had greeted Naomi at the gates of Bethlehem four chapters back and told her to praise God?* Even though it might have been appropriate for Naomi to praise God at both times, a sensitive friend would not demand it in those early scenes. Here the women share Naomi's joy—and direct her toward praise.

**Questions 13, 14.** Pace the study so that you leave time for thoughtful responses from each person who wishes to participate in these questions. If it seems appropriate in your group, ask for question 14 that each person speak a few words of encouragement to the person on his or her right.

**Continuing.** Speak or sing the words of "Great Is Thy Faithfulness." Suggest that people use this song as a prayer, then lead into the guided prayer, using spoken or silent prayer for each listed idea—as seems appropriate for your group.

# For Further Reading

Aharoni, Yohanan, and Michael Avi-Yonah. *The Macmillan Bible Atlas*. New York: Macmillan, 1977.

Alexander, Desmond, David W. Baker, and Bruce Waltke. *Obadiah, Jonah, Micah*. The New International Commentary on the Old Testament. Grand Rapids: Eerdmans, 1988.

Bright, John. *A History of Israel*, 3rd ed. Philadelphia: Westminster Press, 1981.

Buttrick, George Arthur, ed. *The Interpreter's Bible in Twelve Volumes*. New York and Nashville: Abingdon Press, 1954.

Douglas, J.D. *The New Bible Dictionary*. Grand Rapids: Eerdmans, 1962.

Edersheim, Alfred. *Old Testament Bible History*. 1890 Reprint. Grand Rapids, MI: Eerdmans, 1980.

Fee, Gordon D., and Douglas Stuart. *How to Read the Bible for All It's Worth*. Grand Rapids: Zondervan, 1981.

Ferguson, Sinclair B., and David F. Wright, eds. *New Dictionary of Theology*. Downers Grove: InterVarsity Press, 1988.

Finzel, Hans. *Observe Interpret Apply*. Wheaton, Ill.: Victor Books, 1994.

Gorman, Julie A. *Community That Is Christian: A Handbook for Small Groups*. Wheaton, Ill.: Victor Books, 1993.

Guthrie, D., J.A. Motyer, A.M. Stibbs, D.J. Wiseman. *The New Bible Commentary, Revised*. Grand Rapids: Eerdmans, 1970.

Hubbard, Robert L., Jr. *The Book of Ruth*. The New International Commentary on the Old Testament. Grand Rapids: Eerdmans, 1988.

Keil, C. F., and F. Delitzsch, ed. *Commentary on the Old Testament in Ten Volumes*. Grand Rapids: Eerdmans, 1980.

Kuhatschek, Jack. *Taking the Guesswork out of Applying the Bible*. Downers Grove, Ill.: InterVarsity Press, 1990.

Nyquist, James, and Jack Kuhatschek. *Leading Bible Discussions*. Downers Grove: InterVarsity Press, 1985.

Parker, Margaret. *How to Hear the Living Word*. Wheaton, Ill.: Victor Books, 1994.

Plueddemann, Jim, and Carol Plueddemann. *Pilgrims in Progress*. Wheaton, Ill.: Harold Shaw, 1990.

Tasker, R.V.G., ed. *Tyndale New Testament Commentaries*, 20 vols. Grand Rapids, MI: Eerdmans, 1963-1980.

Tenney, Merrill C., ed. *The Zondervan Pictoral Encyclopedia of the Bible*. Grand Rapids: Zondervan, 1976.

Wenham, G.J., J.A. Motyer, D.A. Carson, and R.T. France, ed. *New Bible Commentary: 21st Century Edition*. Downers Grove, IL: InterVarsity Press, 1994.

Walvoord, John F., and Roy B. Zuck, eds. *The Bible Knowledge Commentary, Old Testament*. Wheaton, Ill.: Victor, 1985.

Wilhoit, Jim, and Leland Ryken. *Effective Bible Teaching*. Grand Rapids: Baker Book House, 1988.

Wiseman, D.J., ed. *Tyndale Old Testament Commentaries*, 24 vols. Downers Grove, IL: InterVarsity Press, 1994.

Wuthnow, Robert. *Sharing the Journey: Support Groups and America's New Quest for Community*. New York: The Free Press, 1994.

# Notes and Prayers

# About the Author

Carolyn Nystrom is an eager traveler who loves rapelling in the mountains, wading at the seashore, and hiking over all the land in between. She is also a journeywoman when it comes to studying and understanding God's Word. An author of over fifty books in ten languages, Carolyn has proven herself as an accomplished editor and writer of Bible studies through her work on the Young Fisherman Bible Studies (Shaw); the Women's Workshop  Series and Discipleship Series (Zondervan); the LifeGuide Series and Christian Character Series (IVP).

In her church, Carolyn has taught almost every age, served on a host of committees, worked as small groups coordinator, and proffers wisdom as an elder. In addition to her contributions to her local church, she is a member of her denominational Christian education committee (Evangelical Presbyterian Church).

Carolyn has a B.A. in psychology from Wheaton College and has done additional course work in education, literature, and writing at a variety of universities. She and her husband Roger are the parents of four adult children and two sons-in-law. She lives in St. Charles, Illinois and works as an editor at Victor Books.